An Altered *Yes*

Kiawana Leaf

An imprint of Pen Legacy, LLC, Pennsylvania
www.penlegacy.com

Library of Congress Cataloging – in-Publication Data
has been applied for.

Paperback ISBN: 979-8-9894778-4-5
e-Book ISBN: 979-8-9894778-3-8

PRINTED IN THE UNITED STATES OF AMERICA.

FIRST EDITION

To my children, Azariah and Azir…

Thank you for choosing me, for helping me grow into the woman I am ordained to be, for helping me turn my perceived losses into victorious wins, for pushing me to come into agreement with my assignments, and for giving Mommy the space to be better for you. Mommy loves you both immensely!

Table of Contents

An
Altered *Yes*

The Essence of Key

"Kiawana, nickname Key,
Reaching for all God has for me,
Leaving behind all that is not
God has assured me all I need I already got
When I think about the essence of a Key,
It opens up locked doors, you see
What I haven't seen in the spirit before
I now have the Key, not locked anymore
Free from opinions and how people see what they see
Too busy unlocking the doors He has set before me
God, I am grateful for the gift of Key
I will use it as a light so other young women can be free."

~ Pastor Cleveland Bates

I Got The "Key"

Do you know where the hardest and most uncomfortable place in life is to be stuck? The middle!

You thank God you're not where you used to be, but you're not quite where you desire to be. You're stuck between both; seemingly, you can't break free. It's a tug-of-war. You take one step toward reaching your goals, only to be moved right back to the middle. Sometimes, you find yourself back at the beginning because you like the feeling of comfort in the familiarity.

So how do you let go of what's holding you back?

Take a moment to jot down in a notebook or journal what you think is holding you back from fulfillment. Could it be fear, accountability, rejection, trauma, low self-esteem, finances? What's causing dis-ease where you currently are in life?

Coming into agreement with our assignments means committing our thoughts, decisions, desires, plans, lives, and will to God. If I can be honest with you, it's HARD as heck! I'm sure you will agree.

Can you recall numerous times you've prayed to God, telling Him your wants, desires, and plans for your life? You dreamed of marrying by age thirty and owning a house with a white picket fence and a vast backyard. You wanted to raise your children with your husband or wife—one big happy family. You wanted this or that, this way or that way. Think about it. What prayers have you solicited to God? What plans for your life have you shared with Him without realizing they are not even your own?

Seriously, think about it. I'll wait. Better yet, writing out what you asked for from God may be more helpful. So, go ahead and flip open that notebook or journal again, and write it out.

God, I need this promotion.
God, I must start this business.
God, I want to date him/her. Please make them the one.
God, I have this vision. This is what I want, so You must give it to me.

How many times have you petitioned God for your desires and wanted Him to agree with *your* plans for your life? You looked at Him as if He is a genie waiting to grant your wishes if you rubbed your Bible enough times.

Can you see why I said it could be HARD to come into agreement with your assignment?

Some things you ask for may not be meant for you, and some routes you want to take may not be the paths ordained. Accepting this is the difficult part of coming into agreement, but don't be discouraged. Some things you want may be a part of His will. However, obtaining what you desire won't always be a walk in the park. You'll have to jump through some hoops and avoid some loops in the process.

Are you willing to endure long-suffering, surrender to God, and submit a fresh *YES*?

This means you must take a step back and let go of what you think you want, how you want it, your plans to get it, and the idea of following your own agenda. You must submit to His will and way. This is challenging because His will and way don't always feel good. It may not be easy, and it gets lonely. It's not always exactly what we want or how we envisioned it.

"Long-suffering" is a fruit of the spirit! That can be a whole lesson in itself, but to touch the surface, long-suffering is patience. It requires us to wait patiently without complaining, getting irritated, or becoming angry.

Whew! I had to repent while writing this because I was in a situation where I allowed myself to become irritated and angry. But check this: God doesn't allow anything to happen without a plan or purpose. We often cause ourselves frustration by getting ahead of Him. Okay, I'm getting ahead of myself. Let me bring it back in.

Look back for a second and be honest with yourself. Can you say you received what you prayed for? In other words, are you living an answered prayer?

I used to pray and beg God with tears in my eyes to make me a boy mom. God truly blessed me by answering my prayers to be a mother, and He is still answering many others! However, it didn't happen as I expected or how I wanted Him to bless me: to have a son. Instead, I was blessed with the most beautiful daughter.

A scripture many refer to but don't fully live by is Jeremiah 29:11 (AMP): *"For I know the plans and thoughts that I have for you," says the Lord, "plans for peace and well-being and not for disaster, to give you a future and a hope."*

Let's unpack this!

As I was getting ready for church today, I said, "Good morning, Big Fella! Thank You!" No other words were needed, and yes, this is how I address Him. I talk to God like He's my father, homeboy, best friend, and confidant, but respectfully. I had to develop an intimate relationship with Him that was comfortable for me and no one else. I couldn't talk to God the way they do over the pulpit, nor did I have the same images as others of how He is supposed to look. That didn't work for me. Many are conditioned to talk with and view Him in a certain way. I wanted to have an authentic relationship with God.

Throughout my thirty-plus years of living, we've developed just that—a dope, authentic, genuine relationship. My relationship with God has helped bring this project to fruition to share with you. I had been praying for guidance on how to deliver this book. While trying to come up with the title, God told me to share my story about maneuvering through the middle.

My response? *The MIDDLE?!? It's a mess. It's uncomfortable here. I'm stagnant some days, and other days, I'm propelling. I feel like I'm all over the place. I don't even understand the middle. I'm still trying to figure it out. So what, Big Fella? What, why, and how would You have me deliver to others on being in the middle?*

I was completely flabbergasted! Then I heard Him ask, *Do you trust me?*

This season, my only answer to God is yes. All else has failed me. If I give a fresh yes, submit, obey, and trust in Him, I CANNOT FAIL! Do not be fooled, though. As easy as that was for me to write, it has been hard as hell to live it.

I had been receiving an adequate amount of much-needed confirmation about being in the middle. But to be honest with you, I've been running. It has been HARD! I needed and wanted to be in control. But today? Ohhh, today was a gut puncher. Have you ever been yoked up by your parent, grandparent, or another family member? Or maybe you can recall when you had to yoke up your child because they weren't listening and firmly tell them, "Enough is enough. You better listen to me!" Yep, that's how I felt.

Instantly, I heard Him say, *Being in the middle of perfection and progression.*

Inquisitively, I replied, "Huh, Big Fella?"

Kiawana, you are in a season of knowing what you're not going back to, God told me. *We've grown so much together. It's time to pull back and address the layers you've previously rebandaged, which is the progression. You receiving my promises and being obedient are perfection to me!*

Upon hearing His word, I replied, "Yoooooo, God, that's dope! You're right! I *am* in a season where I'm not going back."

I refuse to settle anymore. I'm not going back to the root of the wound, nor will I continue to hold on to deadly branches. No longer will I go in circles chasing people and things that are not meant for me. My colleague and I like to say we're starting from scratch.

This season is about me. To receive a brand-new outcome, I must do something new. If not, I'll continue to get the same results. Starting anew requires me to submit and obey to receive a different outcome, not drag my feet and question God's will. Delayed obedience is disobedience! Trying to be in control is disobedience! Therefore, I will relinquish control, be obedient, and allow God to guide my steps and instruct me in my actions.

Sounds good, right? Well, it felt good for me to say and write it. I definitely shook my own tables with that one, especially since I am the type who always feels the need to take control.

But how do I stand firm in the middle while progressing when it's so easy to backslide? It's not a fight, it's not a storm, and it doesn't involve strategic planning. It's comfortability! It's familiarity! It's already knowing the outcome—the ins and outs of the process. It's about being in that safe place and space. But, baby, it's easier said than done.

What happens when you don't agree with the process? What if God answers your prayers, but the outcome isn't delivered as expected? What happens when life makes you take a detour, and you must submit while traveling a long, tough, dark, hurtful, lonely, scared, unexpected, and unknown route? Worse yet, what if God simply tells you NO?

Kiawana Leaf

Father, as the reader reads my words, may they hear less of me and more from You. May they step in my shoes but present their story to You to receive a clear message. May Your light shine so bright through me that they have no choice but to surrender a fresh yes to You! I love You and thank You in advance for the souls You have sent to receive Your word— those who need this and are hungry to start anew. Father, I ask that You guide them to an altered yes! May they never delay or cancel their reward because of their disobedience that stems from their pride, ego, gluttony, arrogance, fear, control, or lack of accountability. In Jesus' name, Amen!

Alright, reader, are you with me? LET'S GOOOOOOO!

First, forgive me for not introducing myself sooner for those of you who may not already be familiar with me or haven't read any of my other books. My name is Kiawana, but my friends and family call me Key, and it's a pleasure to allow God's light to shine so vividly through me. My passion is to help those who are lost, broken, or may have been abandoned by their parent(s), significant other, friends, or even their church. I want to be the voice and motivation for those who feel rejected, betrayed, excluded, or like the black sheep. For the strong survivors, single mothers, and brokenhearted who walk around masquerading their pain, I'm coming for you. You are not alone. My mission is to help those who don't understand the purpose of their pain and show them how our consequences are a part of God's plan so that we can be an example for the next man. Revelation 12:11 (NKJV) says, *"And they overcame him by the blood of the Lamb and by the word of their testimony."* So, it is my hope that I empower you to inspire another. Empower Too Inspire®!

I am stuck in the middle, so what's next?

In 2009, I graduated high school and believed I had found the love of my life. Young and naive, I fully gave myself to this young man. Boy, was it a time, and I don't mean in a good way how we use it today.

He did everything right in terms of filling my voids. See, I was raised by a single mother and her husband because my biological father wasn't present in my life how I desired him to be. So, I went searching and accepted the first man who fulfilled my wants and needs that I desperately sought from my earthly father. I didn't know my identity. So, I settled on receiving time, attention, emotional availability, and physical touch, thinking it was enough. Needless to say, this relationship led to my first trauma wound and left me feeling insecure.

Since my dad was inconsistent in meeting my wants and needs as his daughter, I thought it was okay and accepted the same in my relationship. My mother raised me to believe what went on in our home should stay in our home. So, I would walk on eggshells, afraid to express my feelings, searching for a place where I could feel safe to let go and receive all I believed I wanted and needed.

I've shared that so you can know a little about me and get a glimpse of the root of my pain. If you haven't read my first best seller, *Confidence Unlocked*, you should do so. It will give you more insight into my relationship with my father as a child and how it affected my relationships with men when I got older.

I created a vicious, toxic cycle, and in 2021, before giving birth to my son, I had to ask the Lord to reveal myself to me.

I experienced so much hurt, rejection, abandonment, and heartbreak as a single parent and domestic violence survivor, even becoming an abuser. I was hurt by people I knew, loved, and truly trusted, including church members. But God showed me, me!

When asking God to show yourself to you, you must become the two words so many people have trouble being: ACCOUNTABLE and VULNERABLE! But let me tell you, there is so much freedom in the presence of the Lord. To be completely naked and feel safe is an indescribable feeling. Try Him out!

It's much easier to blame the other party, and a

majority of the time, they may have been the person who did some messed-up **S**ugar **H**oney **I**ced **T**ea to you. But what did *you* do to make them think it was okay to treat you in such a way? What self-respect did you lack that they took as the green light? What insecurities did you display? Some of you will argue me down and think that me saying take accountability is victimizing you. If that's how you feel, I can tell you this book isn't the one for you until you're ready to grow up and stop ignoring the three fingers pointing back at you.

Many of us wrestle with our pride and ego, but let's not fool ourselves. You can't step to the Big Fella like you're going to a masquerade ball. You can't dress to impress and cover your face with a mask, thinking you're fooling, playing tricks, or running game on God. You can't throw money at Him—or tithe as the church folks call it—and think He'll tolerate your ish. God will pull you apart layer by layer, piece by piece, to the point where you will legit be naked in His presence! How do I know? I was there. I haven't released a project in the last three years because he was stripping me apart drastically. During that period, I spent time in His presence, trying to figure out my life. I needed to figure out who Key was and find the Key that He called me to be. I had to learn to unmuzzle my voice and break myself free from the shame, guilt, and fear.

Kiawana Leaf

I used to always say it's "Mask Off" season, and I'm picking it back up again because that's exactly what this is — "Mask Off" season!

The enemy doesn't want you to take the mask off because it's easier for him to trick your mind and keep you in the same broken cycle. He doesn't want to see you grow and prosper. But I'm coming to ignite and stir up the fire inside myself and you. It's time to break the chain of the enemy and link your chain to someone who needs the words of your transparent and authentic testimony!

Listen, I know how it feels to take correction and accountability as an offense. But how else do you expect to succeed, learn, and grow? How do you get out of stagnation? How do you think you will receive a different outcome?

What you are doing is not okay, and the way you are living is not right. Most times, you need to be checked instead of being encouraged to continue throwing a pity party for yourself.

I ran away from the pain, trying to trick myself into believing I was okay. I feared the discomfort associated with the pain. Yet, I always found myself in a vicious cycle of craving lust to fill my voids. The scars from my childhood encounters affected my mental as an adult, and my picking at the scab only made the wound bigger than it was in the beginning. Rebandaging my scars with the same ole dirty "aid" left me in a cycle. *Same gift, different package* is a familiar quote that I am sure we've all heard at least once. Commit to asking God to show yourself to you right now.

Now, please don't take what I'm about to say as me being selfish or feel as though I don't care about your struggles, but the truth is, this book isn't for y'all. I have bottled and buried so much inside for the last two years, and this is my release. Still, I want to encourage you by giving you the Key to do so, too!

Something I discovered along the way is that I really am the Key, and you are, too. It's simple yet complicated. However, your obedience and submissiveness are the reason you have the key to open many doors.

Detour (Faith vs. Trust)

Although I have the keys, it doesn't mean I can enter every door. I will be the first to let you know I am not perfect! Again, I am NOT perfect! I AM NOT PERFECT! I am human and have fallen short multiple times. I've stepped out of alignment with God's will, trying to figure it out on my own. And guess what? I FAILED EVERY TIME!

I hear from God, but sometimes it can be challenging for me to understand or receive his instructions. I've come to accept that my Key doesn't fit every door. So, it's up to you to realize and accept that every chapter may not be your best chapter, every door is not meant to be unlocked by your key, and every road may not be a straight shot to your destination. Sometimes, you'll have to take a detour or even sit still until another route is shown.

Have you ever been (or are currently) in a situation

you knew you had no business being in, and you tried (or are trying) to find the answers to make it work or get out? Have you gone to God and said, "Father, You have to make this work. Save him/her. Fix what's broken. I need x, y, and z. Open this door and that door, or so forth and so on?" I'm sure we are all guilty of petitioning to God, asking Him to make something work out. Often times, we get attached to people, places, and things that aren't even assigned to us. In some cases, He's protecting you from something because you're not equipped to handle it. Or He allowed a situation to break you in order to make you! Now with that last one, you may be saying, *"God allowed it to happen? What do you mean, Key?"* Well, let me tell you.

He's God, and He can easily pull you out of any situation, remove people from your life, or do whatever else is necessary to keep you from enduring hurt, pain, disappointment, etc. But, if He did it instantly, would you still seek Him and consult with Him?

No! You know you wouldn't. We would keep doing what it is we were doing and expect Him to move and make something happen on our behalf. That's how we begin to abuse our grace and mercy. But when we maintain our faith and endure the trials, we learn to greatly appreciate and embrace our growth, grace, and mercy of which God has blessed us.

Oftentimes, our posture becomes wrong in His presence. We get upset, frustrated, and anxious because things aren't happening the way in which we desire them. God's not answering our prayers because He's not moving how we expect or want Him to. We don't appreciate the process of our consequences because we lose control and must fully submit. Mmm, there goes that word "control" again.

That's when you have to LET GO! If you don't, you'll allow your flesh to believe it's His spirit that's your desperation and leading you to destruction.

I won't allow my flesh to misconstrue His presence as being my desperation that leads me to destruction! Highlight this, tweet it, write it on a Post-It Note and stick it on your mirror. Do whatever that will help you to remember this.

We have to die to our flesh DAILY, meaning give up some of our worldly ways. But mighty lamb of God, it is NOT easy! Yet, it is so rewarding!

I had to learn to give the Key (myself) over to God and allow Him to use me in the way that He rightfully deserved to and desired. I'm not the Key that I used to be, but I'm also not the Key that I ought to be if I were to be completely honest, transparent, and raw with you. Obedience is better than sacrifice. How do I know? I have experienced both the rewards of being obedient and the sacrifices of being disobedient.

I charge you with this question: *What are you using your key for?*

We are going to travel on this detour together. Is that alright? Do you use your key for what you want to do and how you want to do it? Even when you don't understand, do you still submit and unlock what God has assigned for you to do? Do you make the sacrifice to unlock a door by faith? Or are you just unlocking doors because you got the key?

"It's true that our freedom allows us to do anything, but that doesn't mean that everything we do is good for us. I'm free to do as I choose, but I choose to never be enslaved to anything."
1 Corinthians 6:12 (TPT)

I used my key to do what Key wanted to do, living in my wilderness and attempting to enjoy life while gliding through "obedience" when I knew better. I continued on like this until God literally sat my tail DOWN and made me be still during my detour. I believed my pride and ego could change or help save someone. I thought I could be their savior and pull them up and out of their pit. I would get attached in ways I had no business getting attached to them, when my capacity was to only be an assignment led them to God and then release them. You

An Altered Yes

have to know and understand assignments vs. attachments.

I created attachments from my assignments to fill voids and insecurities within myself. I thought I was doing the right thing, but using my wisdom, discernment, and looking back now, I have to say to myself (in my best Madea voice), "Girl, Kiawana, you were dumb as hell!" What can I say? I was selfish and wanted what I thought I wanted.

Have you ever realized how the scales that impede your vision fall off of your eyes after the fact? Have you ever felt like that before? I'm sure many of us, if not all, have looked back on a situation and said to ourselves, "If only I knew then what I know now" or "If only I would've seen this before." But most times, we did. We just chose to ignore the warning signs because it— whatever "it" was—felt good in that moment. We made the mistake of letting our pride and ego trick us into believing we could make something work that wasn't meant to be.

I am now BIG on accountability. I haven't always been, but where I am, I made the conscious decision to look at my reflection in the mirror and accept responsibility because it all starts with self.

Ignoring the red flags, I believed I could make my situations right. My pride and ego got in the way. One of the things God ABSOLUTELY hates is a prideful and egotistical person! Little did I know, my pride and ego would quickly crash and result in me experiencing immense guilt, shame, regret, and embarrassment.

"Instead of your shame there shall be a double portion; instead of dishonor they shall rejoice in their lot; therefore in their land they shall possess a double portion; they shall have everlasting joy."

Isaiah 61:7 (ESV)

So much gratitude for my last season forced me to spiritually grow up. With my faith and God's strength, He pulled me out of my own pit—a pit where I felt like God was punishing me. He was ashamed of me; I was such a disgrace. I felt like He took His hands off me— removed me from His table and cast me into a sunken place where I muted my voice and stopped moving in His glory. I honestly was ashamed to call myself a Christian, but I got myself up faithfully to meet him in His place.

I didn't feel worthy. I hid behind my guilt and shame, burying myself in the broken pieces while trying to fix my bad decisions. I was afraid to bring my filth to Him. Situations can no longer be embarrassing unless you are embarrassed by them. There's only one way to rid yourself of guilt, and that is to face it! By working through my feelings of guilt, I was finally able to see my value. It is also what led me to my first detour.

I feared being a single mother again. I had invested too much time, emotions, finances, and energy into this relationship to just walk away. Honestly, I had no business getting into it to begin with, but it's too late to think about that now. Again, I didn't want to be the single mother times two and was worried what people may say or think! People pleasing and being our own worst critic can be our biggest downfalls. Even before my life reached that point, I feared being alone, desiring so much to be in a relationship that I was willing to settle and accepted mental and emotional abuse. I found myself being buried in my own pit of condemnation, shame, guilt, and conviction. Believing this was my punishment for conceiving a child in a messy situation, I STILL tried to do things my way without consulting God.

I remember talking to one of my sisters, and she asked me, "Key, how are you?"

"Girlllllll, do you really want to know?" I replied. "To sum it up, I'm trying to stay above water to keep myself from drowning!"

To this day, her response resonates with me when life seems to shake the tables.

"How do you expect God to save you if you keep fighting against Him?" she told me. "You won't LET GO for Him to dive in and rescue you. It's just like a lifeguard. A lifeguard can't save someone who is fighting against the water and them while panicking to save themselves. If the lifeguard was to dive in then, they would either both drown, or the lifeguard would have to make the decision to let the person go to save themselves, and the other person may end up still drowning. But if that person were to have faith and stop fighting against the help, they would be able to be saved. The same applies to you and your situation. The lifeguard 'God' can rescue you before you go too deep, but you have to stop fighting against His help."

Whew! That was quite a word! Breaking down into tears, I vowed to myself that I would totally surrender myself to Him, agreeing and accepting His will and plan for my life despite not knowing what to expect.

I remember telling Him, "Father, I'm letting go. Only You can save me. I'm tired of panicking, fighting against Your will and way, and trying to figure it out for myself. I don't have the strength left to fight a battle that doesn't belong to me. Trying to have control is burning me out completely. I know that you want me to be postured in the right position to accept and ask for Your help. No, I don't only want Your financial blessings. I want and need Your strength to be able to endure this season of transition."

However, as I was journeying through this detour, I realized it wasn't my lack of faith that was the problem. It was my TRUST with Him that I struggled with.

We're on a detour, right? There's a lot of traffic and roadblocks that we are going to hit, so we have time. Let's unpack this! Define what faith and trust are to you.

If you are like me, you probably thought those two words meant the same thing. When you look up the word faith, trust is included in the definition. As well, when you look up trust, faith is listed there. I am sure you're thinking there isn't much of a difference. But there is, and that's where we mess up. Let me give you a couple examples that pertain to myself:

♦ I had all the faith (belief) in God that He would carry me through, but my trust (commitment) was faint.

♦ I had faith (believed) that a lifeguard would come and save me if I'm drowning, but I didn't have much trust (commitment) in the lifeguard that when I let myself go, He would come and save me.

Do you see the difference? It's not my faith I struggled with; it was my trust. My faith (belief) is there, but my trust (commitment) is faint.

Y'all, I had NOTHING! I lost everything going against God's will, but still having to trust Him with my transition and seeing nothing was HARD! Struggling with my guilt, doubt, fears, and insecurities made it hard for me to trust God. After experiencing so many detrimental situations, my trust was nearly non-existent. I was afraid to let anyone in, and quiet as kept, I was afraid to let God in, too.

"God, these here are your people," I remember telling Him. "So, because your people hurt me, I struggle with fully committing to You."

I told you before I really talk to God like he's my homeboy, but the most amazing and beautiful thing is that God is NOT like man. He isn't. You may feel it is cliché for me to say, but until you actually experience what it is I'm telling you, you won't fully understand.

Just because…I'll just call him Jaquan…robbed me of my peace, broke my heart, abandoned me, and left me depleted, it doesn't mean God will. And He doesn't. I have expectations of what life should be and how it should flow, but my life is not my own. Yes, it is completely and perfectly fine to have expectations. You should. After all, you are human. Just because you are a Christian doesn't make you a robot with no emotions or feelings. However, does your expectations align with

God's will for you? Sometimes it's tough to accept that your expectations are not what He has planned for you to receive. When He alters your expectations, will you still tell Him yes?

There is purpose in pain, and pain births purpose! That is one motto I live by and stand firmly on. It is NOT easy, though!

You. It's you that's in your womb. The shift in your life that you weren't ready for is the woman inside of you that I ordained you to be. Not only did I give you my son to birth for you to move, but it's also time for you to give birth to your promises because someone else is depending on you to see and hear me to be free.

Crazy, mind blown, stuck, gazed. I don't know how else to describe that moment God randomly spoke to me.

You ever find yourself constantly pondering on the why and the purpose of whatever your "it" is? For me to birth the bold, fierce, and authentic woman that's inside of me, I had to lean on prayer, fasting, worship, my faith, and intimate moments with God to build my trust.

If you're someone's birth mother, then you are familiar with the rough times experienced during pregnancy and labor, such as back pain, uncomfortable feelings due to the pressure of carrying your child, not being able to sleep, and the excruciating feeling of contractions and having the urge to push. Although necessary in order to help move the baby down into the birth canal, the contractions are brutal and at times unbearable. However, some women are given an epidural to numb the pain. Giving spiritual birth is totally different. There isn't any medication to ease that pain.

Just as a natural birth, spiritual birth is the greatest transition or shift of your life. You become a mother with natural birth, and you become all who God has called you to be with spiritual birth. While both transitions can be exciting, they do not always feel good. The pain and discomfort from the weight gain, swelling, contractions, betrayal, rejection, abandonment, unexpected loss, loneliness, and unfamiliarity can be overwhelming.

I had every reason to be stressed, depressed, lose my mind, throw the towel in, and turn my back on God, but because I remained steadfast in my faith, I was able to maneuver over those speed bumps into joy and peace. I fully understood who I was ordained to be and the force that I have in God's kingdom. No, it didn't mean life still wouldn't life. However, I would be able to handle life lifing a bit different.

If you don't know your identity, you will be a lost cause and crumble whenever the slightest pressure is applied.

I've accepted that many obstacles I faced were

because of my own doing. Sometimes I found myself enduring unnecessary struggles, but eventually, I became comfortable with being uncomfortable while moving in obedience and my faith. No, I didn't always get it right. I made mistakes and still do. Many obstacles were my fault because of my disobedience and wanting to use my "key" Key's way. That's when I realized it wasn't that I didn't trust God. I didn't trust myself with trusting God wholeheartedly.

As I mentioned earlier, one thing that has been my downfall is feeling like I always needed to be in control. I made the mistake of thinking Key could do it Key's way. By that, I mean trying to hold on to a relationship past its expiration date. Due to the actions of my child's father (or rather lack of actions), I found myself unemployed for a year. For twelve whole calendar months, I had no source of income coming in. I'm getting teary-eyed thinking about it now. Still, even in my foolery and disobedience, God kept me. I didn't deserve His grace and mercy at all. I intentionally ignored His word, making myself an idol and believing I could do the impossible. Truth is, I was a fool to think I was stronger than Him and go against His instructions for me to let my relationship go. If I had listened to Him, I'm sure I could have avoided that period where I felt unsupported, unappreciated, and unloved.

But who would want to let go of something they initially prayed for even though they did not receive their ideal mate? Becoming a single mother again is not what I imagined at this stage of my life.

During my time of being unemployed, my car never got repossessed. My children and I still had a roof over our heads, food on the table, and clothes on our backs. We did not lack for anything. I can wholeheartedly, proudly, and boldly testify that God has been Jehovah Jireh, my provider. Jehovah Shalom, the Lord, is my peace through it all.

I need you to understand that I didn't get this peace of mind by suppressing what I felt. I can relate to the emotional stress some of you may be feeling. I get it. Trust me, I do. I remember picking up the bottle to ignore the pain. I remember smoking four to five jays a day, trying to escape my reality. I would have sex to experience that feeling of being wanted and stay in relationships just to say I had someone. All those things were temporary fixes.

This time around, it was different for me. I went through the motions and felt every emotion. Some days, I screamed and sobbed in the shower, and there were plenty of nights when tears soaked my pillow as I cried myself to sleep. I got frustrated with my situation. I was upset that despite all my efforts, I became a single mother

An Altered Yes

again. I was angry and humiliated about being lied to by someone I would have given everything to. I felt like I was suffocating from the anxiety, hurt, and grief. I expressed all this to God, my spiritual leaders, and my village. Then you know what I did next? I let it go!

I would be lying if I told you everything was peaches and cream after that. My later shift was filled with many lessons, trials, and tribulations that I believed were punishment, but that detour was actually preparation. Faith and forgiveness were the two weapons I used to pull me through, with forgiveness being the hardest. Dealing with the rejection that drew me closer to His acceptance made the weight of forgiveness a bit easier to carry, but I still struggled with it and became depressed.

Pain produces pressure that births purpose. This was all the rebirth of Key, becoming who God called me to be, and I'm growing daily to be the woman who was hiding behind my shame and guilt.

I'm here! I got my voice back. I pulled my seat back up to the table and started building more for myself. Don't remove yourself from your seat at God's table because of perceived losses. If I don't leave you with anything else, please know that God keeps His promises, and you STILL belong.

We have the nerve to give up on God. Yet, He doesn't give up on us despite all our flaws and shortcomings.

God isn't like man. He'll NEVER reject or abandon you, leaving you high and dry like man. He doesn't turn on you or forsake you. He doesn't talk about you, lie to you, love bomb, gaslight, manipulate, or abuse you physically, mentally, or emotionally. God isn't a narcissist.

No matter how far you think you've gone, you can always come back to Christ. There's no mistake He can't forgive and no sin that's too big. He's waiting for you with open arms. You're deserving, you're worthy, and you are loved. God won't drop you; rest in that. There's safety in Him! He's a good, good Father! There is none like Him.

While redefining my worth, I developed more value and appreciation for myself during my transition on this detour. Not only was I beginning to trust God, but I also started trusting myself.

The devil thought I was going to stay down. He thought he could keep my voice muzzled. He desires and bets on that for all of us, but God is merciful. He's a God of grace and a Father to the fatherless. Trust that it will all work out for your good. Keep your eyes on His promises for your life, and don't be distracted by what you see today. As long as you still have breath in your body, it is not the end. He still has a need for you, and everything you go through is NEVER just for you.

An Altered Yes

"Look away from all that will distract us and focus our eyes on Jesus, who is the Author and Perfecter of faith [the first incentive for our belief and the One who brings our faith to maturity], who for the joy [of accomplishing the goal] set before Him endured the cross, disregarding the shame, and sat down at the right hand of the throne of God [revealing His deity, His authority, and the completion of His work].

Hebrews 12:2 (AMP)

When preparing to give birth to my son, I remember saying, "In a few weeks, I'll experience a NEWNESS of life and love!" In that moment, I was speaking of my baby and finally being a part of the boy-mom gang. After beginning the process of letting go, I received prophetic word after prophetic word, so much confirmation. I knew the Lord was 'bout sick of me! But prophetically, I was speaking over me, although I didn't fully understand everything I was saying. There's indeed power in the tongue!

As mothers, we stop living solely for ourselves and start living to care for and nurture our children. We stop working for the first three months after giving birth, lose sleep, can't eat this, won't do that, et cetera, et cetera. But through all its ugliness and beauty, motherhood is so rewarding.

If I can be transparent with you, I lost my voice when

I found out I was pregnant. I hid in the shadows of my shame. I was legit upset with God. He knew the desires of my heart, and that wasn't it. I always wanted a son, but I wasn't ready. I know what some of you may be thinking. I thought the same. Yes, I'm a Christian, but I'm also human, which makes me imperfect. I can be the first to admit my flaws and not barricade my skeletons in the closet. Those bones might help save the lives of those suffering in silence.

To be honest, you can get defeated by valuing people's opinions more than God's approval and acceptance of you. I did, and because of that, I struggled. I valued people's thoughts more than God wanting my submission through this. I wasn't in agreement with God's will, and I felt ashamed. Only God can give life, and He makes no mistakes with His works. This detour was one that I needed to take to fully understand this very thing.

So, when I say I'm back, it's personal. And I owe God everything. I'm getting back in alignment with God. I'm STILL chosen, and I am still LOVED. I am unlocking my confidence once more, and so can you! This year has truly taught me that it's okay to start again. Life will humble you to the point where you will have no choice but to start again, and that is okay. But we must also recognize our flaws, repent, and submit to God during the process. I am so grateful to God for His protection, provision, strength, peace, joy, grace, and providing for me during my last season. I am giving Him the rebirth of Key, and those Keys are opening locks to a lot of newness. The devil should've killed me when I didn't have a voice because I am now unstoppable in my faith.

God's choice is for imperfect people to accomplish the impossible with His perfect power!

What you're going through is hard as hell, but the only thing that can break hell is heaven! The beauty of it all is that we are ALL imperfect people. He's just waiting for your Altered Yes to be perfect in His image!

Detour II
(Construction, You)

"And whoever comes to me must follow in my steps and be willing to share my cross and experience it as his own, or he is not worthy of me. Those who cling to their lives will give up true life. But those who let go of their lives for my sake and surrender it all to me will discover true life!

Matthew 10:38-39 (TPT)

"You never pick right when you pick from pain." How many of you have heard that saying before? That quote has so much truth, and I can share why I firmly believe so. Although it's a bit easier for me now to submit an altered yes since the transition, I've struggled a lot and had to take several detours to get here. Often, we become desperate and want to be in control, independent, and strong. We look for a quick fix and feel everything must

go our way. We can't stay down too long; we don't want to go through the process. We want what we want NOW without having to wait. Let's call a spade a spade. We don't want to go through and experience pain. Why would we? It surely doesn't feel good. But if we were honest with ourselves, most of us would agree we cause our own pain, which is caused by our impatience and refusal to relinquish control.

I'm sure you petitioned a prayer request to God like…

"Okay, Big Fella, any day now. I'm tired of waiting. Why does it have to be this way? I asked for this, but You gave me that. I wanted it like this, but You gave it like that. You said You would never leave me nor forsake me, but where are You? Do you hear me? Can you see me? It wasn't supposed to be like this. I didn't ask for it this way. I trusted You to fix it, but it has gotten worse. I asked You for healing, but You took life. I asked You for a family, yet I'm a single parent. I asked You for a better job with more money, but I'm still stressed. I asked You for spiritual healing, yet my soul still feels depleted. I'm empty behind closed doors."

We put expectations on too many people who aren't capable of meeting our needs. How many of you can relate? We ignore the warning signs. Instead of letting go, we try to figure it out to make it make sense when we've already seen that it doesn't. We have all asked God for something, and His delivery wasn't always what we expected. Or maybe He straight-up told you NO. What's your response/reaction when life makes you take a detour?

Detour: a different or less direct route to a place that is used to avoid a problem or to visit somewhere or do something on the way. Example: You'd be wise to make/take a detour to avoid the construction. (Cambridge Dictionary)

The example given is good for the context of this book. However, I would prefer to say, "You'd be wise to take a detour to avoid *construing* the construction." It may not make sense to you now, but I promise it will one day. If you haven't already, go ahead and highlight that sentence. I'll be referring back to it often.

Father, I don't always agree, but I love You and Your words! I pray as I try to unpack this how You've given it to me that I'm able to help free myself and someone else from the weight of the disappointment from their expectations. I feel tired. I feel the weight. I feel the burden. I feel the disappointment. I feel the loneliness and the brokenness, too. I have been trying to avoid the detour—the shift—and have become frustrated with You

47

because it isn't the route I expected to take. Before I go any further, forgive me for putting myself before You, resulting in anxiety from not understanding the construction of my life. I'm responsible for the unnecessary weight I picked up to carry. Help me release the weight and understand that this is the route I must take and that the construction is You building me up for a better life. God, I love You, and I thank You!

Take a moment to be honest, transparent, authentic, and vulnerable with yourself. No one knows your thoughts and prayers but you and God. Collect them in your mind. I'll give you a minute. Now, write down your prayer requests, thoughts, feelings, and desires in this moment.

You'd be wise to make/take a detour to avoid the construction. That's the sentence used in the Cambridge Dictionary as an example for the word *detour*. I examined this sentence deeply. I became intrigued and eager to unpack and apply this to my life piece by piece. I kept hearing and seeing the word *detour*. I would dream of detour signs, construction trucks, hazardous materials, roadblocks, and a beautiful outcome from the construction. I asked God, "What are you saying? Why are you showing me this?"

You're probably wondering why I would define *detour* as if you didn't know. I thought the same thing when God gave it to me. Don't think I'm trying to insult your intelligence. I'm sure you already know the word's basic meaning, but I need you to look at it outside of a natural-eye perspective.

No, detours are not only inconvenient delays that prevent you from beating the initial arrival time your GPS calculated when you typed in your destination. You set your sights on taking a particular route because it will get you to your destination quicker than another way, but not viewing life from a natural-eye standpoint will cause you some heartache and pain. You have to be open to changes during the journey.

We often become too comfortable in the familiar. I'm guilty of this. I didn't want to make any changes, but at the same time, I felt neither satisfied nor complete. So, I had to change what was familiar or stay stuck in that unhappy place with my pride and ego as my company.

God, I thank You for this revelation. We only call on Him when faced with a problem and forced to take a detour. Our plan didn't work as expected, or there was an issue on that route. We didn't think we would hit bumps along the way, but now that we're here...

I tried to do it on my own—in my own strength, in my own power, and in my own way. I stuck with what was familiar, but none of it was working.

"Hello, are you there?" I asked God but got no answer.

I knew then that I had to take a detour. I had to venture on an unfamiliar road because of the renovations taking place up ahead that I could not yet see.

You'd be wise to make/take a detour to avoid the construction. That is the example I told you to remember, but can you recall my interpretation? You'd be wise to make/take a detour to avoid *construing* the construction.

How many times have you found yourself driving and ran into a detour? I bet you said, "Ugh! This is going to make me late. They are always doing construction on these roads." Or maybe you've said, "Oh God, not another apartment!" You found some reason to complain, and the road rage instantly kicked in.

What if you'd be wise to make/take a detour to avoid construing the construction? What if you were able to see the beautiful things from the construction just by taking the detour? What if God is trying to make you understand the meaning of "beauty for ashes" but you must take this detour to get there?

Have you realized that the construction is you?

This detour (or shift) frustrated me because I wanted things to be smooth sailing and fit my expectations. However, I'd be wise to make (or take) the detour (or shift) to avoid construing (or misinterpreting) the construction (process). In other words, I would be wise to submit an altered yes.

We're never postured right when maneuvering from pain or trying to escape/avoid the pain, difficulties, errors, and unfamiliarity. You'd be wise to go through the process. It's impossible to survive without God's grace.

With the first detour, we learned the difference between faith and trust—how it's important to defer the two to God and yourself. But what happens when you hit a roadblock? I'm glad you asked.

I found myself crying many nights, succumbing to my feelings of inadequacy, anxiety, anger, fear, frustration, and depression. Believing I was unworthy and undeserving, I lost my confidence and voice. *Lord, why do people abandon me when my heart towards them is always pure? Why must I always get the short end of the stick? I take five steps forward only to be pushed twenty steps back. Why does my life have to be like this?*

I had so much anger and animosity towards God during my process because He said in Jeremiah 29:11, *"For I know the plan I have for you, plans to prosper you and not to harm you, plans to give you hope and a future."*

"Then why is this place heavy and dark?" I would cry out. "Why am I constantly crying and ready to quit? Why am I hurting, broken, and depressed? This is not peace but surely a disaster. WHYYYYY? I despise it here. This wasn't my plan. This wasn't what I asked of You! I didn't ask You to do this like this!"

Did you recognize my error? Can you see how I sort of got myself tangled up? Can you admit that you've done the same thing once before? Can you be honest and say you didn't trust God or yourself? Or maybe you made the mistake of only looking at the end and not considering the process to the promise.

I asked you before to write your prayer requests, thoughts, feelings, and desires. Well, here's another opportunity to do so. Let this be an intimate moment between you and God.

When expressing your requests, thoughts, feelings, or desires, did you say to God that whatever His plans are for you, your answer is yes? Did you tell Him that whatever His will is for your life, may His will be done? Be honest. I'm guilty of my answer being absolutely not, so don't be ashamed if you answered no. I told you how my conversations went with Big Fella: *Lord, fix this relationship. Lord, I want a son. God, I need income. Lord, heal my father. Lord, do this; God, do that. Lord, I need or want this or that. You got to make this work, God. Save me like this, Lord.*

The Lord never said He agreed with me or that my plan for my life was better than His, and therefore, that's what He would let it be. Based on Jeremiah 10:23, I know our lives are not our own. We are NOT able to plan our own course. So, correct me, Lord, but please be gentle.

Do not correct me in anger, for I would die.

So, your favorite preacher could be leading you astray by telling you to submit your plan to God as if it's His plan for your life. We put limits on Him, demanding to be pulled out of our pit that we created for ourselves. That right there is already a big mistake.

When we should be turning to God, some of us choose other means for dealing with our painful situations. Some use alcohol as a crutch to escape reality. Others abuse marijuana to numb the pain. Then there are those who go from relationship to relationship, thinking it will heal their hurt or fill the void of loneliness. And let's not talk about the ones who bury themselves in work to keep their mind occupied to avoid facing the truth. We don't want to take the detour because it's longer than desired or expected, but … "You'd be wise to make/take a detour to avoid construing the construction." No, taking the detour won't always make us feel good. I thank God for not being a God of feelings, meaning He doesn't move based on how He feels. Would we still be here today if He did?

Do not correct me in anger, for I would die!

What if God responded to us the way we respond to Him when things do not work out as we imagined them? Bask in that for a moment.

The process, this "construction", the building up of

one or something. You! We prolong or miss the purpose of it by ignoring the detour signs, wanting to go our usual route instead because of what we are accustomed to, what may feel good, or what may seem like the easy way out. We look at the construction and believe God is angry with us. So, we take matters into our own hands. As a result, we create worry, stress, depression, and pain for ourselves. We lose our faith and trust in God. We think we are experiencing punishment rather than correction to build us up.

Now, you can choose not to keep it real with yourself, but you're going to keep yourself in bondage with that mentality. As for me, I can be completely transparent and authentic. That's the only way to be free. By running in shame and guilt, you will go the opposite way than the route God has already ordained for you to take. You will find yourself moving further and further away from God, which is what the enemy wants. The enemy is determined to keep you drowning in insecurities and low self-esteem.

You'd be wise to make/take a detour to avoid construing the construction. The construction is YOU! Not only did I free someone with this word, but I also had an epiphany and freed myself. Enjoy the detour to become a better you!

Unforgiven Entanglements

Desperation will make you lose focus of your desires and neglect your discernment. At times, we try to fix broken relationships, ignoring the sharp pieces and not realizing how deep the cut is until it's too late. How many times have you told yourself to give it one more chance but knew you should've walked away? Deep down, I knew it wouldn't work, but I wanted it to work. I had to make it work because I had invested too much time and energy. I felt like I had to prove to myself that I could have a long-lasting relationship. Have you ever ignored your discernment to fit what may have been comfortable to you at that moment? You felt in your gut that it was wrong but repeatedly prayed to God to make it right.

I remember hysterically laughing while talking to God and saying, "At this point, Big Fella, if I'm meant to be a customer service rep for your people, just say that!"

I was not prepared to be chin-checked.

"I never called you to that," He replied. "That was the road you chose to take."

I was FLABBERGASTED! God surely shook some tables when He told me that.

I would rather pour out and give help than receive help and complain to God. I always wanted to lead, but I was never called to be the leader in certain situations. Yes, a healing spirit attracts broken people, but don't make the mistake of thinking you can lead them all.

You can't save everyone, Kiawana, I would tell myself. Everyone isn't supposed to be attached to you, Kiawana. You're trying to control situations you can't control, Kiawana. You are trying to change people that you can't change, Kiawana. Demons are NOT going to like you, Kiawana, and that is okay. You are NOT God! You are going in circles because you want situations to work out how you want them to, and some situations aren't even meant for you, Kiawana.

Now, reread that, but replace my name with yours. Read it aloud. Let those words marinate for a minute.

Did a light bulb light up? Now, what I'm going to tell you to do next will sound crazy, but do it anyway. I wish I could see you actually try this, but…

Look at your back.

Yes, I said look at your back!

Go ahead. Do it.

I don't think God would outright call us stupid, but I am sure that's exactly how you felt while trying to look at your back. You probably looked stupid, too. Wouldn't you agree? *chuckle*

You may be wondering where I'm going with this. Well, the point I'm trying to make is to stop attempting to do things that are impossible for you.

You caught yourself tangled in this fantasy world, and now you're frustrated because you feel as though you have failed yourself. You may feel like a failure because you had an expectation you were not capable of achieving. You are heated with someone because they won't do what you want them to do. Or maybe you are angry with God because He didn't do what you wanted Him to do when you wanted Him to do it or how you wanted Him to do it. I know I struck somebody's nerve with this because it struck me, too, when I was traveling along this detour.

In a sense, I became an idol of myself, and honestly, you are, too. How? Because we have been out of line and want our plan to work. We do not accept, agree with, or be in sync with the purpose already written for us. We have extreme admiration, love, or reverence for our *own* will, way, and plan. That equates to IDOLATRY!

Kiawana Leaf

"Many plans are in a man's mind, but it is the Lord's purpose for him that will stand (be carried out)."

Proverbs 19:21 (AMP)

God did not say that particular man or woman was meant to be your husband or wife. You were the one who wanted that, but it didn't fit. God did not have that job assigned to you, but you wanted it anyway. That wasn't His purpose for you; that was the plan you set for yourself. Now, out of desperation, you jump at the first opportunity or commit to the first person who crosses your path because you are trying to fill a void instead of showing patience and waiting for what God has coming down the pipeline for you. It may not happen as fast as you would like, but trust me, it will be better than settling for something that doesn't compare to your purpose.

The biggest thing we lack as people is ACCOUNTABILITY. But in this season of my life, I can't start from scratch without admitting where I have been wrong and then repenting, denouncing, and casting it to God.

God, please forgive me for idolizing myself and thinking I was greater than You. Father, I denounce what I settled for because I felt You were supposed to be on my time and make it work. Father, forgive me for the sins that I came into agreement with that were not a part of Your purpose for me. I denounce every word cursed that has been formed against me and spoken about me by my enemies. There is still a purpose over my life greater than the plan I had set for myself. You said in 2 Corinthians 12:9 that your grace is sufficient; your power is made perfect in weakness. So, here I am—still worthy, still deserving, and still who You called me to be! Amen!

I want to share something with you about myself in just a few, but before I do, I want you to complete something. Think of this as another journal entry for the day. It doesn't have to be long. However, I want you to complete it. Deal?

In 3-5 sentences, write a reflection on how you see yourself. When you look in the mirror, what do you see? And no, I'm not referring to your outer appearance. So, none of the "I am beautiful, thick, wealthy, and independent" self-praise that strokes your ego and makes you feel good. Seriously tap in and write a reflection on how you see yourself.

I know part of my purpose here on Earth is to help heal the brokenhearted, and throughout my previous dating experience, I often found myself getting attached to my assignments when it came to men. But after that last one, baby! I don't need any more lessons.

You never pick right when you pick from pain.

Where did your need to be strong and independent derive from? What was the root?

I had no choice but to be strong and independent, especially becoming a single mother after the birth of my daughter. Yes, I have my core—or a village, as some would say—that supports me. However, my child is not my core's responsibility. Having a child by my abuser placed me in a different mental and emotional bondage that I wouldn't wish on my worst enemy.

I kept thinking to myself, *Kiawana, why are you still doing the same and picking from pain?* But still, I did. I thought he was different. Not only did I think he was different, but I also saw potential in him. Can we be honest and admit we have fallen for someone's potential? Or, if you have the gift, you saw who God created the person to be...if only they would surrender and do the work. I saw who God created him to be, but let me tell you something. Seeing the potential in a person more than they see in themselves will cost you. You will lose so much! Mentally, spiritually, emotionally, physically, and financially, you can lose it all!

Now, not everyone will make immediate moves towards becoming who God intended them to be, but at the same time, don't ignore the red flags of stagnation because you want to fill that empty space. Make sure they have goals for their life before you begin to share your life with them. Don't allow them to bring you down or hold you back. If it doesn't make sense, make an exit.

Trust me on this. I know from experience. I lost it ALL!

My first red flag was a clear sign. There was so much confusion, and my spirit wasn't at peace, but I had to make it work. While running from my demons and hiding behind my scars, I accepted A LOT of situations I internally couldn't even stomach. Key, the people fixer, to the rescue, but who was there to rescue me?

What happens when the empath falls in love with the narcissist?

When you haven't fully healed from your inner wounds, you don't see or accept yourself as God sees you. You're gullible, vulnerable, and wide open. A narcissist preys, feasts, and gets a thrill from your type. I was once that type. They spread your nose wide open and get you right where they want you so they can abuse and manipulate you. Then, when you've had enough, you're the one who is blamed for the dissolution of the relationship instead of the violator owning up to the part they played.

As I mentioned earlier in this book, we, as humans, lack accountability and try to avoid being vulnerable. We are quick to point our index finger at someone but ignore the three pointing right back at who? Yup, you. But, on this detour, I looked at myself a lot in the mirror. I didn't ignore those three fingers, and I constantly beat myself up, my anger rising inside of me like a tidal wave. Still, even with all the pain and hurt I felt, I continued to pray for God to make it work.

It was never my plan to be a single mother yet again. Hell, it wasn't the plan the first time. Not taking the time to build a solid friendship before falling headfirst in love clouded my judgment. I found his emotional availability in the beginning very seductive. He wooed me with date nights, trips, and gifts. Being able to communicate in a healthy manner, show attention, and spend quality time together was something I had desired in my relationship, and he gave it to me. However, challenges began to arise when he started feeling vulnerable during moments of real intimacy. The more I asserted my desires and wants, the more disconnected and distant he would become, resulting in more arguments and fights. Again, I would pray, "God, fix it. Please make it work."

I asked you to write a reflection on how you see yourself, and I hope you took the time to do so. Allow me to share with you my reflection of myself:

I see myself as someone who has been hurt a million times and then some. I see a lost, broken girl who's trying to figure it out but is running in the opposite direction. I am full of rage, regret, and resentment. I am plagued by guilt and shame. I am timid, hiding in my mistakes and feeling insecure, unworthy, undeserving, and like a failure.

While wiping away the many tears I cried constantly, I would ask, "God, why am I here yet again?" I would beat myself up, thinking I made the wrong decision to have a baby in my current situation. Why didn't I walk away in the beginning? WHY? I remember feeling frustration, irritation, regret, disappointment, and anger—all of which I kept bottled up and tried to hide behind a smile. Then, one day, I finally found the safety to release it, and I have no one but God to thank for pulling me out of it.

It sucks having a heart of gold and attempting to do right by people only to be left empty. I grew tired of getting the short end of the stick or receiving leftovers in return for the love I gave so freely. Despite the many reasons I had to have a bitter heart, I couldn't do it. Still, it doesn't mean I wasn't left frustrated and fighting to heal from broken relationships—romantic, platonic, and business.

How do you forgive someone who's not even sorry? On this detour of unforgiven entanglements, I had to forgive myself first. As I journeyed through, I realized my unforgiven animosity wasn't towards the people who hurt me. I was withholding forgiveness for myself.

Without forgiving myself, I found myself in the same broken patterns while attempting to create something new. But that's impossible to do if you're still holding on to an unresolved grudge within you. Self-forgiveness is a must!

Everything starts within you, and I realized the saying "you are what you attract" is very true. I found myself dating people who were ashamed of their past traumas and sins. They were toxic, insecure, and full of regret. Everything legit reflected me. Attempting to operate in my oil, I still tried to be the empath, showing them love and grace because I knew I would need it along the way myself. Then, finally, I decided I'd had enough. I refused to keep doing this to myself. I would not continue to be entangled with the same demon with a different face. I refused!

So what did I do? First, I had to forgive myself. I was the one hindering and holding me hostage in those entanglements. I forgave myself for thinking I needed to fill the lonely void along this journey. I forgave myself for thinking I was a failure because I couldn't save everyone. I forgave myself for being afraid of thinking and being different. I forgave myself for being ashamed of being different from the culture. I forgave myself for making myself an idol. I forgave myself for trying to step ahead of God. I forgave myself for trying to be the author of my own story. I forgave myself for causing more harm to myself because of my refusal to let go. I forgave myself for settling for less than I deserved and thinking I had the power to punish myself because of my sins, flaws, and all. I forgave myself for hurting myself. I forgave myself for thinking I wasn't worthy. I forgave myself for looking at myself as less than what and who God called me to be. I forgave myself for how I viewed myself after experiencing all my trauma, pain, and shame.

This may have been easy for me to write, but truth be told, getting to this point of forgiveness for myself wasn't easy and took me a while to achieve. But I chose to do it. Being able to fully forgive yourself requires compassion, empathy, kindness, and acceptance—whether you're trying to work through a minor mistake or one that tremendously impacted not only your life but also the lives of those connected to you, such as your children, parents, spouse, significant other, or whoever. All of us make mistakes. It's inevitable. After all, we are human. We are imperfect people, but you can choose to be better and do better.

Here are seven keys that helped me along on this journey of my unforgiven entanglements:

Kiawana Leaf

1. **Focus on your emotions.** I gave myself the space and grace to feel what I felt, and I wasn't afraid to petition God for it. I grew deeper in love with God by just being honest and authentic with Him. However, most of the time, we try to hide behind our emotions by saying we're okay or doing things to suppress them instead of giving ourselves permission to recognize, accept, and embrace our feelings.

2. **Acknowledge your mistakes outside of your thoughts.** You know how you may be too ashamed of the mistake to speak about it, so you keep it trapped inside? Nope, I had to hold myself (here goes that word again) ACCOUNTABLE. I acknowledged my mistake aloud and what I learned from it. Then, I let it go. Keeping your thoughts silenced will only muzzle your voice, creating inner turmoil.

3. **Look at every mistake as a tool from which to learn.** I took the time to learn what I liked and didn't like, what I would and wouldn't accept, how I felt, and what I didn't want to feel like. Holding the key to my mistakes propelled me forward.

4. **Put your journey on pause when you need a moment.** It's certainly not a race, and you have to go to the beat of your own drum. As long as you're putting your best foot forward to reach your goal, don't pressure yourself. Oh, and please don't make the mistake of running back to what's familiar during your pause. Growth is painful but necessary.

5. **Show yourself some self-compassion.** This journey was unfamiliar to me. So, I was going to make mistakes, and no, I wasn't going to always get it right. I had to learn to be gentle with myself. That way, I would never settle for anything less than how I treated Key. I would silence my harsh inner critic voice and quickly shut the negativity down, giving myself grace in this unfamiliar place. Our thoughts can be a hinderance to forgiveness. It's time to show yourself some compassion and grace. The best way is to be nice to yourself. Learn to love your interior before the exterior. This takes time and patience, and this process is one I don't think will ever end. Many days, I still have to remind myself I am worthy of forgiveness.

6. **Take your own advice.** I became my own patient, if you would say. We often give so much to others that we forget about ourselves and become depleted. It's easier to tell someone else what to do, walking them through the steps, than to take your own advice. I told you that ACCOUNTABILITY and VULNERABILITY became my two best friends. Let them become yours, too.

7. **Stop reliving the mistake.** Reliving my mistakes only kept me stuck in a pity party and stagnation. It's okay to process your mistakes, but do not keep replaying them. Baby, I was famous for doing it. I would fast forward and move beyond my mistake, only to press rewind and find myself drowning in it again. When I caught myself feeling ashamed, I would renounce the thoughts and reaffirm to myself that I had already overcome those times.

Remember the exercise we did earlier when I asked you to write down how you see yourself? Well, open up that notebook or journal, and let's try it again. This time, write a self-compassion response for what you wrote before.

Forgiveness is essential to your healing journey. It allows you to let go of anger, guilt, regret, shame, fear, or anything else holding you back from moving forward. Once you release yourself from your own condemnation, you'll begin to experience freedom. Are you eager to apply the keys on your detour to an altered yes? I hope so.

From Scratch – Transition from My Hands to Yours

In this unfamiliar place, stand firm in letting go. Release things from your hands to God's and bask in letting go of things you can't control. I accepted long ago that everyone isn't for me, and I'm okay with that.

Learn to hold yourself accountable instead of basking in a vicious cycle. Trust yourself more and stop being your own worst critic. Forgive yourself just as Christ has. Accept that you are a son or daughter of Christ. Stop rehashing the hurt and let go of the pain. Break free from the bondage and become anew. You will surely bloom!

To achieve the aforementioned, you must do it in the spirit and not of your flesh. You must fully submit and commit. When you understand that life decisions aren't solely to be viewed with your natural eye but also your spiritual eye, you will weather the storm differently.

Let me tell you, the attacks I've endured to get this book out, plan for my nonprofit annual community baby shower, maintain my love life, and heal from my wounds have been vicious! One thing about me, I will never share anything I have not experienced or applied to my life. My purpose is to be a living example, showing you that you are worth it and He is worthy to do it!

Everything we encounter is not always the enemy. God uses our broken pieces to grow us, build our character, and strengthen our trust and faith in Him. No, it doesn't feel good and isn't always pleasant. However, one thing is for sure—we weren't ever promised an easy life. If you can find a scripture where God promised us that life would be easy, I will remove this book from every platform it will reach. A promise He does make to us is that the weapon formed against us will NOT prosper.

God often leads us into mental, emotional, spiritual, and physical desolation, and oftentimes, we mistake it for punishment, loneliness, and/or rejection. But we must remember that God never allows anything to happen in our lives without a plan and a purpose.

Let me say that again!

God NEVER allows anything to happen in our lives without a plan and a purpose!

Rest in that for a second. Write it down, make it plain, and grab a hold of it.

The problem begins when we misconstrue the detour. We try to make sense of and take control of the plan or purpose that He has already written. We get in our own way and block God from having His way. Our pride, ego, desperation, and hunger lead us in the wrong direction. Instead of being selfish, we must become selfless, submit, and repent.

While we are here, I think this is a phenomenal place for some self-deliverance to set yourself free. Let go of what's holding you back and step into your new.

Say this prayer with me:

Father God, I humbly enter Your throne in complete vulnerability. I stand before You completely naked for You to search me, oh God. I welcome You into this space to make me anew. Father God, I love You, and I honor You. I bow and clothe myself before You with Your grace and mercy.

Lord, forgive me for getting in Your way. Forgive me for thinking I am mightier than You. I repent of my sins for becoming my own idol—thinking, believing, and reverencing my ideas, plans, and purpose are greater than what You have already written for me. I repent for my fleshly desires that got me caught up in making wrong decisions. I release myself from all relationships that You did not ordain. I release myself from all thoughts that were not Your thoughts concerning me. I release myself from the vicious cycles that I have remained in until now.

Father, I break free from the enemy's captivity and escape the road they laid out for me. The detour had gotten too long, and I became impatient. But today, I repent and confess my wrongdoings for lacking faith and trust in You. Father, I ask for Your forgiveness for turning away from You because You didn't move when I wanted You to or do what I wanted You to do.

Father, I enter Your throne with forgiveness in my heart. Thank You for loving me. Thank You for keeping me. Thank You for forgiving me. Thank You for never letting go of me. I am still here because there is more. So, Father, I honor and adore You. I pour out to You. Father, the going may get rough, but You tell us in 1 Peter 5:7 to cast all our anxieties, cares, and worries upon You because You care for us. So, Father, forgive me for using coping mechanisms instead of turning to You. I release myself from fornication to fill a void. I release myself from excessive drinking to escape reality. I release myself from excessive smoking to numb the pain. I release myself from all soul ties that pull me away from You.

You are a good, good Father, and I thank You. I am free! I am free! I am free! Father, you told me in Micah 7:19 that all our sins have been cast into the deepest part of the sea, never to be retrieved or brought up again. So, Father, I release myself from my own captivity. I release myself from repeating the same cycle You have already forgiven me for. Father, thank You for the woman (or man) that I am becoming. Thank You for thinking I deserve to become her (or him)! Father, I thank You!

If You can forget my sins, then why can't I? I release myself from the enemy's trick to convince me that You don't love me or think I am deserving. God, I vow before You and commit to being who You ordained me to be. Father, search my heart and help me on this detour. Thank You for the keys to guide me through the tests, trials, and tribulations. Thank You for giving me the strength to survive the season I am in and fully submit to You, Father, so I can be prepared for what may come. Let Your will be done, not mine.

Jesus, I thank You for another chance. God, I thank You for another chance. Abba, I thank You for another chance. Thank You for always providing for me. Thank You for healing my body. Thank You for keeping my mind, God. Thank You for overlooking Your blessings for me because I was too caught up in myself. Less of me and more of You, Father. Less of me and more of you, Father. LESS OF ME AND MORE OF YOU!

I exalt Your name, oh God. There is none like You, and I thank You for being better than good to me. God, I release myself from my own condemnation, which keeps me separate from You and holds me back from reaching my full potential. Today, I am hopping off the merry-go-round and walking this thing out with You, Father. I renounce every cursed word that has been spoken over my life. I am free from all captivity. I am made a new creature.

Father, I confess my sins. I am a sinner who is asking for Your forgiveness. I turn from my sins and invite You into my heart. I want to trust, obey, and follow You as my Lord and Savior, Father, and friend. There is none like You!

Kiawana (insert your name), I forgive you for your sins. I forgive you for your childlike ways. I forgive you for trying to figure it out the best way you thought was right. I forgive you for not trusting yourself. I forgive you for thinking less of yourself than what God called you to be. I forgive you for thinking you had failed. I forgive you for your wrongdoings and past mistakes. Just as God, I cast my mistakes to the bottom of the sea and will not allow anyone to remind me of my past wrongdoings. 2 Corinthians 5:17 tells us that being in Christ, we are a new creation. Old things have passed away. I am made anew. I have a new life and a new identity. Thank You, Father, for the freshness and newness of life! Father, remove anyone from me who wants to keep me captive and surround me with the right core to uplift, support, and encourage me. Surround me with righteous people in tune with You so I may walk the path to Your light.

Father God, we honor and thank You. In Jesus' mighty and most precious name, we pray and praise. Father, heal and save souls to glorify Your name. God, we all have a story. We all took a detour and got stuck, Father, but may we surrender to You to uplift our brothers and sisters to enhance and glorify the Kingdom. God, I thank You! I love You, and I honor You! Thank You for another chance. Thank You for Your grace. Thank You for Your mercy! I don't deserve it, but You see fit. I am so grateful that You qualified me for the call. Father, I honor You and bow before You in your Holy matchless name. It's in Jesus' name that I decree and declare freedom over my life. I declare freedom over every reader's life in Jesus' name. Father, may we bloom. May we be set on fire for You! I love You, Father. I love You, Father. I love You, Father. Thank You for my brothers and my sisters who are reading this book. Father, although this book was set for my freedom, may someone else be free just by reading it. May they totally surrender to you, God. In Jesus' name, Amen!

I dare you to serve the enemy notice TODAY that you are free! I dare you to shout aloud, *"Satan, you should've taken me out when you had the chance! I escaped, and I am made anew! God got me! I submit to the King, not to you!"*

Then turn your attention to God and say, *"I thank You for your plan and purpose, Father. Thank You for opening up my spiritual eyes. Thank You for raising me higher. Hallelujah, God! I thank You! We are victorious people. We know no defeat in You! I transition from my will to Yours. I start from scratch and allow You to be God. I let go, Father. I let go, Father. I totally surrender."*

My appointed time is now. I bloom forward in the name of Jesus. I bloom past all distractions. I bloom past everyone the enemy set against me. I bloom over my enemies. I bloom into my destiny and purpose. I bloom from a place of lack into a period of abundance.

I am healed from being left. I am healed from bad decision-making. I am healed from cursed words spoken over me. I am healed from adultery. I am healed from abortions. I am healed from church hurt. I am healed from dysfunctional families. I am healed from bitterness. I am healed from disobedience. It all ends with me, and a newness blooms within me. There will be pressure, tests, trials, and storms, but I have the keys to win through grace, peace, joy, and laughter. My survival days are OVER. I bloom in everything that my hands touch. I bloom in every room my feet land. Father, they may have left and rejected me, but they couldn't kill me.

I will not rehash the pain. I will not sabotage my future. Father God, thank you for Your grace.

I feel God moving. You may not see or believe what I'm telling you, but apply the keys I have shared. Submit to His spirit, not your flesh. Romans 7:18 (NKJV) tells us, *"For I know that in me (that is, in my flesh) nothing good dwells."* As well, Romans 8:4-6 (NKJV) says, *"that the righteous requirement of the law might be fulfilled in us who do not walk according to the flesh but according to the Spirit. 5For those who live according to the flesh set their minds on things of the flesh, but those who live according to the Spirit, the things of the Spirit. 6To be carnally minded is death, but to be spiritually minded is life and peace."*

"My flesh and my heart fail; but God is the strength of my heart and my portion forever."

Psalms 73:26

The Middle is the End

"There shall be no more pain, for the former things have passed away. Behold I make all things new. Write for these words are true and faithful. It is DONE! I am the Alpha and the Omega, the Beginning and the End. I will give of the fountain of the water of life freely to him who thirsts. He who overcomes shall inherit all things, and I will be his God and he shall be my son."
Revelations 21:4-7 (NKJV)

You may be wondering how the middle is the end. Well, let me explain. It's because you now have the keys that will prevent you from going back to the beginning if you use them. You've escaped what's familiar. But even if you do backslide, don't be hard on yourself. Remember, we are human and not free from erring. I pray that you stand firm in your boundaries; however, getting to the middle will take some practice. I refer to the middle as the end because the weapon will form but not prosper.

Kiawana Leaf

Throughout life, you'll be tested with your tribulations. How you will persevere through them is the real question to ponder.

Take a moment to acknowledge your progress. You've reached the end of the vicious cycle, and so much more goodness is waiting to be experienced! Let's goooooooo!

As I wrap this up, I pray you hold on to the keys. Remember to take some time to reflect on and release what may be holding you back from reaching your middle. Is it your mindset? Is it the way you see yourself? Do you often refer to yourself as a failure who is unworthy and undeserving? Be honest with yourself. Be completely transparent and naked before the Lord. Repent of what you've made an idol. Renounce what you've accepted about yourself that isn't from or like God. God does all things well! If you feel a situation in your life is not in your favor, let me tell you something. God is NOT through with it yet!

When God gives life, He gives it abundantly. *(John 10:10)* When He gives a burden, it won't be anything heavy, ill-fitting, or more than you can bear. *(Matthew 11:30)* When He welcomes the weary, He'll give them rest. *(Matthew 11:28)* When He frees us, we are free indeed. *(John 8:36)*

I promise you that He does all things well. However,

82

we have to get out of the habit of looking at things through our lenses. We must truly commit to him and submit with our spiritual eye.

I love you, and I hope and pray this book blesses you. I hope it has given you the keys to handle your tests, trials, and tribulations differently to get to your next. I pray it cleansed your lenses so you can view your purpose and assignments differently. I will see you soon with more because there's always more. In the meantime, keep thriving and surviving through Christ!

www.ingramcontent.com/pod-product-compliance
Lightning Source LLC
Chambersburg PA
CBHW060348130626
46553CB00003B/1139